Some Greek Poems of
Love & Wine

SOME GREEK POEMS OF
LOVE AND WINE

being a further selection from
the Little Things of Greek Poetry
made & translated into English

by

J. M. EDMONDS
Lecturer in the University

CAMBRIDGE

AT THE UNIVERSITY PRESS

1939

CAMBRIDGE
UNIVERSITY PRESS

University Printing House, Cambridge CB2 8BS, United Kingdom

Cambridge University Press is part of the University of Cambridge.

It furthers the University's mission by disseminating knowledge in the pursuit of education, learning and research at the highest international levels of excellence.

www.cambridge.org
Information on this title: www.cambridge.org/9781107554313

© Cambridge University Press 1939

First published 1939
First paperback edition 2015

A catalogue record for this publication is available from the British Library

ISBN 978-1-107-55431-3 Paperback

Contents

TO
'Q'

Preface

Readers of my former volume will not expect an Introduction to this. It may be as well, however, to note here that Greek drinking-songs often have other themes than drink—which is why so few of the little poems I have translated are what is generally meant by Bacchanalian. There is no doubt that most of them were sung, or written as if to be sung, over the wine. Now Alcaeus sings 'Wine is a spy-hole unto man', and Plato puts his great word-portrait of Socrates into the mouth of a friend who is tipsy. Perhaps then it is by no accident that these poems give the clear reflexion they do of the old Greek outlook, so childlike and yet somehow so very wise.

A few of these translations were first printed by Mr Peter Davies in *Some Greek Love-Poems* in 1929, one by Mr Heinemann in *Lyra Graeca* in 1927, and one by the Clarendon Press in the *Oxford Book of Greek Verse in Translation* this year.

I wish to thank all my critics for their kind words, and especially one who wrote that he now wished he had learnt Greek.

J. M. E.

10th March 1939

And wine that maketh glad the heart of man.

The Psalmist

Archilochus

The spear 's my bread, the spear 's my wine,
The spear 's my couch when I would dine.

Mimnermus

1

What would Life, what Pleasure, be,
Golden Love, withouten thee?
May I die when none of these
Charms me—shy love-passages,
Suasive love-gifts, the love-bed,
Flow'rs of youth for man or maid;
For once let Eld an entrance win,
Who makes us foul outside and in,
Then Care frets heart unceasingly
And Sun no more delighteth eye;
Hated of child, despised of wife,
Ill hap is his that hath long life.

2

Harm not thou thy fellow-men,
Sojourner nor citizen,
And take thy fling; hard neighbours still
Will speak of thee, some well, some ill.

Mimnermus

3

I sweat and tremble when I see
The glad and glorious flow'ring-time
Of the good men that grew with me,
And wish it longer; youth's dear prime
Lasts as long as dreams a-dreaming;
O'erhead hangs Age, hard, cheap, ill-seeming,
Age that dims what Prowess lit,
And blinds our eyes and blunts our wit.

Sappho

I

TO APHRODITE

[A Fragment]

Come, Love, and mix with dainty cheer
In cups of gold Thy heav'nly wine,
And pour out for our comrades here,
    Thy comrades and mine.

1: *The* wine *is perhaps metaphorical and the poem introductory to the* Book of Wedding-Songs; *if so, the* comrades *are the brides and bridegrooms.*

Sappho

2

Let dainty fingers, Dica mine,
With wreathen dill thy love-locks twine:
For that which is with flowers gay,
Favour never saith it nay;
But she will turn away her head
From all that goes ungarlanded.

3

The Moon is gone
And the Pleiads set,
　Midnight is nigh;
Time passes on,
And passes; yet
　Alone I lie.

Solon

No wealth of silver or of gold,
Of horses, mules, or fields of wheat,
Surpasseth his whose goods all told
Are ease of belly, sides, and feet;
That 's riches; nothing more than this
Goes with dead men down to Dis:
Death will come whate'er you pay,
And aches and age will have their way.

A 2

Alcaeus

1

[*A Fragment*]

Let 's drink; why wait till lights come in?
 The day hath but an inch to run;
Lad, take the great cups from the bin,
 For Semelè's immortal Son
Gave wine our rising cares to quell;
 Be our cups mix'd two parts to one,
And chase each other round pell-mell.

2

[*A Fragment*]

Douse thy weasand well in wine,
The Dog will soon be o'er the line;
Now the Summer 's at his worst,
 And all the world 's athirst.
The artichoke 's a-blowing now
And cricket sings atop the bough;
Now woman wears her sauciest mien,
But man grows languishing and lean;
For Sirius brings a sapless drouth
 On knees as well as mouth.

---

1 *The* cups *of wine are drunk like our loving-cups, that is they are handed round for each guest to take a drink. It was not usual in Alcaeus' day to drink wine neat, nor to carouse before evening. Great* cups *were reserved for great occasions.* 2 Sirius *is the chief star in the constellation of the Great* Dog; *the date is about the 15th July. The flowering of the* artichoke *was with the Greeks a sign of the approach of the Dog-days.*

Athenian Drinking-Song

I

[BY ALCAEUS?]

From the shore your course survey
   To see if you 've the skill to make it;
Once the sailor 's under weigh,
   Whate'er the wind his sail must take it.

Cleobûlus

A RIDDLE

The father 's one, the sons a dozen
   Who each twice-thirty daughters cherish
Whereof each white has one black cousin,
   All immortal, yet they perish.

Ibycus

Love once more looks tenderly
From beneath dark eyelashes,
And with his magic manifold
Will cast me, as he did of old,
Into the snare whence none may fly;
I swear that these assaults of his
Give me to quake like an old champion-horse
That yet again must pull the chariot to the course.

CLEOBÛLUS: *Year, months, days, nights; riddles were one of the forms
of after-dinner entertainment; the poem is rather doubtfully ascribed.*

[5]

Demodocus

The Chians are crooks, not two straight to one wry 'un,
But all—except Procles, and he is a Chian.

Theognis

1

'T is truth, too much wine 's bad; don't blink it:
But if with knowledge men will drink it,
Wine 's not so bad as some would think it.

2

Play on, my soul; soon other men
　　Will see the day;
And I shall be a dead man then,
　　And mix'd with clay.

3

Poor fools are they that drink not wine
When the Dog-Star 's o'er the line.

4

The fairest thing 's uprightness, health the best,
To have our heart's desire the pleasantest.

DEMODOCUS: *The translation omits 'Thus also spake Demodocus'.*

[6]

Theognis

5

If that thou love me and thy heart be true,
Love me not with thy lips but through and through:
Either be purely mine or make an end;
One-tongue-two-minds is better foe than friend.

6

To get and breed a man is easier done
Than to put sense into him; to devise
Means to make bad men good and blockheads wise
Is past our practice; if the leech had won
Pow'r o'er ill nature or infatuate wit,
He 'd earn high wages for the good he 'd do us;
For could good sense be made and put into us,
A good man's son would ne'er go to the devil,
He 'd be taught better. Nay, the truth of it
Is that, by teaching, good ne'er comes of evil.

7

Friends are many o'er cup and platter,
Few when it comes to things that matter.

8

Sons of men, take my advice,
While thoughts are brave and youth 's in flower,
That 's the time to enjoy your dower;
Heav'n gives none his heyday twice,
But ugly Age all heads doth bare,
And Death was never known to spare.

6 Probably by a later hand.　　　　*8 By a later hand.*

[7]

9

With evil spirits twain man's drinking 's curst,
Dire Drunkenness and strength-destroying Thirst:
My way, good friend, betwixt them winds about;
I 'll neither drink too much nor go without.

10

No man, once he 's underground
    And lodg'd with dim Persephonè,
Has joy of flute's or zither's sound
    Or of the Wine-God's charity:
While legs are light and head unshaking,
That 's my time for merrymaking.

11

No wine is pledg'd me now; nigh my sweet Nell
    There sitteth one not near so good as I;
    'His health in water' is her father's cry:
And so she weeps her way home from the well,
    Thither where I so oft have kiss'd her hair
    And she made love's own music in mine ear.

12

To be *in* drink when others are *out* is a sin,
But it 's sin to be out when others are in.

---

10 *By a later hand.*   11 *No name is given in the Greek. It is supposed to have been the custom to drink confusion to a man in water.*

Theognis

13

For joy of youth I play; the time will come
    When, underground, far from the lovely light,
I, good man though I be, shall lie stone-dumb,
    And see no more for ever and a night.

Anacreon

I

Boy, bring the jug; I want a wet;
    Five parts wine, and water ten:
I mean to play the toper; yet
    Topers can be gentlemen.

*   *   *

Let 's give this barbarous boozing up,
    This clamorous after-dinner clatter,
And take a mild and modest cup
    'Twixt pretty songs on themes that matter.

2

Whose after-supper tattle 's ever bent
    On fights and frays, he 's not the friend I choose;
But he that minds him of true merriment
    And mingles Aphrodite with the Muse.

1 *It is not certain that these stanzas ran continuously.*   2 mingles
Aphrodite: *sings not-too-proper songs.*

3

My jowl 's gone gray, gone bare my head,
My teeth are old, and fair youth fled:
Sweet life has but a span to go,
And oftentime I cry me woe
For fear of what Death has for me;
Dire 's his dark hold, and rough will be
The road thither; but worst of all,
Once down, I 'm down beyond recall.

4

TO A DISDAINFUL WOMAN

Thracian filly, tell me why
You look askance when I come nigh,
And flee unkind, as though I knew
Nought of how to manage you?

Should it please me, truth to tell,
I could bridle you right well,
And take and ride you hand on rein
Up the course and down again;

And if instead you graze your fill
And frisk it in the meadow still,
'T is but because a man like me
Knows how long to leave you free.

4 *The last two lines are partly conjectural.*

Anacreon

5

I 've supp'd on a crust of barley-cake,
　But a rundlet or more I 've drain'd of wine;
And now the dear delicate lute I take
　And sing at the door of sweetheart mine.

Athenian Drinking-Songs

2

This is the acorn the sow has got,
　But 'that I should like' says she;
This the fair maid that falls to my lot,
　But that is the maid for me.

3

I would I were a jewel
　Lovely, large, and new,
And a lovely woman wore me
　Whose heart beat ever true!

4

Much is not for mortal man;
Just love and meat and a pull at the can.

5 *The name of the* sweetheart *in the Greek is corrupt; it is perhaps*
Poliagrè. 　　*The metre is intended to suggest that of the original.*
4 *The last five words are conjectural, the original having been ousted*
by Ameipsias' parody.

Athenian Drinking-Songs

5

Would we could open every breast
The heart within to read,
Then close it up and know for sure
Our friend was a friend indeed!

6

Quoth the crab to the snake that he gripp'd in his claw,
'*Go straight and not crooked* is friendship's law.'

7

When I want to be merry with me merry be,
And drink when I 'm drinking with roses array'd:
When I want to love *you*, is the time to love *me*;
Be wild when I 'm wild, and staid when I 'm staid.

8

'Neath every stone a scorpion lurks;
Beware him or he 'll sting:
'T is odds there 's guile and all its works
In any covert thing.

Simonides

I

A MOCK-EPITAPH ON A RHODIAN POET

Your guttling o'er, your tippling done,
You 're lying still, Timocreon.

6 *I.e. the pot once called the kettle black.*

[12]

Simonides

2

He that the sum of happiness would claim
Must choose a native-land of honour'd name.

3

[*A Fragment*]

'T is said Achievement dwells on a rock both steep and high
Where a pure quire of Goddesses
Their watch have set,
Nor may she e'er be seen by a mortal eye
Before we 've shed heart-wasting sweat
And won to the top of manliness.

4

A MOCK-DEDICATION TO ZEUS

Take, Saviour, this from Sôsus and Sôsò
For saving Sôsus' life and Sôso woe.

5

AN AFTER-DINNER IMPROVISATION

Of that which Boreas bold and keen,
Who gripes the guts of ill-clad wight,
Comes south to clothe Olympus in
And then they bury, dead or not,
Fill me my share; for 't is not right
To hand a friend his bumper hot.

5 *This is a riddle of which the answer is snow, which was stored
underground and used by the ancients to cool their drinks; the servants
had forgotten to cool the poet's.*

Simonides

6

'Of like race with the leaves is human kind,'
Thus sang the Chian singer, and sang truth;
Yet most that hear it keep it not in mind;
For hope in each young bosom quickeneth,
And all so long as live the flow'rs of youth
There 's much to our light thinking hath no end;
No more we reckon by old age nor death
Than by disease when we' re in health and strength.
O what a wretched fool is man, my friend,
To reckon so, nor mark the meagre length
Of youth and life! So learn, now thou art gray,
To tell thy soul what she would have she may.

Timocreon of Rhodes

O how I wish, blind Money-God,
No sea you sail'd, no land you trod,
But spent your days on Acheron's bank
   Where dead men go!
We human kind have you to thank
   For all our woe.

6 *The* Chian singer *is Homer.*

[14]

Anonymous

I

[ASCRIBED TO HIPPÔNAX]

Two days are the best of a man's wedded life,
The days when he marries and buries his wife.

*

Anonymous

2

A RIDDLE

Look you at me, I look at you again;
    You look with eyes; I look without; I 've none:
If 't please you, I speak voiceless; all in vain
    My lips wag; I 've no voice, though you have one.

*

Anonymous

3

A piper may have wits from God on high,
But only let him pipe, and off they fly.

2 *A mirror.*

[15]

Callistratus

My sword in a myrtle-spray I 'll tie,
  Like the Great Two
  Who the tyrant slew
And gave our home her liberty:

Dear Harmodius, art thou dead?
  Nay, thou 'rt at rest
  In the Islands Blest
Where Achilles lives and Diomed.

My sword I 'll tie in a myrtle-spray,
  Like the Great Two
  Who Hipparchus slew
On great Athena's holy-day:

Dear Aristogeiton, thou 'lt be known
  Till time shall end,
  Thou and thy friend,
Whose swords gave Athens back her own

Anonymous

4

[ASCRIBED TO THALES]

Plenty in word 's no sign of wit;
Choose text like wife and cleave to it,
Or you 'll ne'er douse the flame you 've lit.

CALLISTRATUS: *The great song of the Athenian democracy.   There seems to have been another version beginning 'None was e'er born at Athens, who...', and in the above the second stanza sometimes came first. 4 This and the following five songs, ascribed to the Seven Wise Men, who flourished about 590 B.C., are probably no older than 500.*

[16]

Anonymous

5

[ASCRIBED TO SOLON]

Be wary, and mind with whom you mingle,
　　Lest smiling front hide armèd back,
Lest double tongue be ta'en for single,
　　And white without within be black.

Anonymous

6

[ASCRIBED TO CHEILON]

Proof of gold 's by touchstone had;
In men 't is Time tells good from bad.

Anonymous

7

[ASCRIBED TO PITTACUS]

When 'gainst the evil man you go
Ne'er forget to take your bow;
Who hath a double-dealing wit
Ne'er opes his mouth but he lie with it.

E

[17]

C

Anonymous

8

[ASCRIBED TO BIAS]

Where'er thou sojourn seek to please;
Who 's kind to strangers hath his ease;
Ofttime stiff presumptuous ways
Fan misfortune to a blaze.

Anonymous

9

[ASCRIBED TO CLEOBÛLUS]

Boors and babblers thick do lie;
Enough 's enough to satisfy:
Use your wits for worthy thought,
Nor let the graces go for nought.

Plato

I

TO ONE CALLED ASTER OR STAR

Star-gazing Star, would I were heav'n above,
To look with many eyes upon my love!

Plato

2

I throw the apple; if thou love me true,
Take it and give what willing maidens do;
But if thy thoughts be other than I pray,
Take 't all the same and think how things decay.

Asclepiades

1

TO HIMSELF

Drink, lad. Tears? Why, what 's come o'er you?
  Love has many a captive led,
And whet for many his shaft before you:
  Why lie down ere you be dead?

2

A fledgling Love, I went a-roving,
  Still easy caught, from Mother's nest,
But from one roof I 'll ne'er be flying,
  And that 's the roof that I love best:
For here both lov'd they are and loving,
  Their well-mix'd wine one cup doth brim;
Each with each in fondness vying,
  None can come 'twixt her and him.

PLATO: *An* apple *was the customary love-gift.*   ASCLEPIADES 2:
For the roof that I love best *the Greek is* Damis' house; *the idea is*
'*first love lasts longest*'; Mother *is Aphrodite.*

Asclepiades

3

'T is sweet to the thirsty in Summer to drink of the mountain snow,
And sweet to the sailor when Winter is o'er the Crown doth show;
But sweetest it is when two have found shelter beneath one plaid,
And the tale of love 's in the telling betwixt a man and a maid.

4

Wine ho! 'T is but an inch from daylight's end;
    Wait, will you, till the lamps 'Good-night' have said?
Let 's merry be; the day 's not far, my friend,
    When they will say 'A long good-night' instead.

5

AN INVITATION

Demetrius, go to market
    And get me at the stall
Three haddock (not too large, please),
    Ten mackerel (mind they 're small),
Two dozen prawns (he 'll count 'em),
    And come back straight, will you?
Oh, and six wreaths; and as you pass
    Ask Tryphera to come too.

---

3 The Crown: *the constellation; ships were mostly laid up in the three winter months.* 4 & 5 *The bringing-in or lighting of the lamps was the mark of nightfall; carouses, for which wreaths of flowers were worn, took place in the evening.*

Asclepiades

6

Ye garlands that with tears I 've wet
   (For lovers' eyes are big with rain),
Stay o'er the gate where ye be set,
   Nor haste to shed your sweets in vain.

But when ye see him ope the door,
   Then show'r them o'er him, every leaf,
That so at least (I ask no more)
   His golden hair may drink my grief.

Callimachus

I

TO CONOPION

As on your threshold cold I lie,
I pray you sleep as ill as I;
Pity me? not a-dreaming, you,
   Though your gentler neighbours do;
Yet when your hair turns gray, you 'll mind
How you play'd me so unkind.

Callimachus

2

Here lies Callimachus, who could both sing
And o'er the wine-cup laugh at the right thing.

✠

Anonymous

10

AN EPITAPH
[ASCRIBED TO SIMONIDES]

Mother of grapes, all-soothing nurse of Wine,
Whose crinkled withes a random trellis twine,
Climb o'er this little mound, and top the stone
Which marks the grave of old Anacreon;
So the fond friend of thy sheer liquor, Vine,
Who thrumm'd the lover's lute in night-long mirth,
Shall yet sport o'er his head, though lapp'd in earth,
Thy branches' glorious bounty ever new,
And have eternal unction of the dew
That erst perfumed those agèd lips benign.

---

10 *The poem clearly belongs to a later time, when these 'fancy-epitaphs'
were fashionable.*

Anonymous

11

Fair, Persian mothers, are the babes ye bear;
Yet Arimazd is fairer than the fair.

Posîdippus

I

FOR AN EPICUREAN CLUB-DINNER

Show'r upon us, Attic flagon,
    Bacchus' all-refreshing dews;
Give our tongues good stuff to wag on,
    While as no man's guests we meet.

Hush'd be sage and swanlike Zêno,
    Mum be old Cleanthes' Muse;
Let our theme be things that *we* know,
    Love and how he 's bittersweet.

❧

1 Zêno, *the head of the Stoic school of philosophy, lived to be* 98, *dying probably in Posîdippus' lifetime;* Cleanthes, *who succeeded Zêno at his death about* 260 B.C., *was probably his contemporary; in* swanlike *the reference is perhaps to his pertinacity in continuing to teach the Stoic principles of moderation when he was considered past his work. Cleanthes wrote a famous* Hymn to Zeus *which is extant* (Oxford Book of Greek Verse, 483).

Posidippus

2

Dip the ladle, Heliodôrus—
          one dip each will do for us—
First for Nanno, second Lydè,
          third the wise Antimachus,
Fourth Mimnermus, fifth your servant,
          sixth—say 'Lovers the world o'er.'
Love, a bumper! drunk or sober,
          this for me is all your lore.

Antipater of Sidon

I

AN EPITAPH

I know not whether to complain
Of Bacchus' wine or Zeus's rain;
Both for the feet are treacherous:
Here Smyrniot Polyxenus,
Returning whence he 'd been to dine,
Slipp'd and fell; the moral mark,—
When you 've had your fill of wine,
Beware wet footpaths after dark.

---

2 *Each ladleful poured into the cup represents one 'toast'.*   *The two lines, probably interpolated, adding a seventh, eighth, ninth, and tenth, for Hesiod, Homer, the Muses, and Mnemosynè, are here omitted; the 3rd line is clearly the climax, nor are Hesiod and Homer poets of love. Nanno was Mimnermus' flute-player and mistress, Lydè Antimachus' wife; both poets called a collection of love-poems by their ladies' names.*

Antipater of Sidon

2

AN EPITAPH

You that pass by Anacreon's simple grave,
If you 've had profit of those books of mine,
Let wine's dear sacrament my ashes lave,
That these cold bones may feel the warmth of wine;
So one that erst of wine's sweet lore drank deep,
Once wine-fond Music's foster-brother, still
Shall have wine's company whene'er he will,
E'en in the land where all their tryst must keep.

Anonymous

12

A wet kiss, as the twilight fell,
  Came from a pretty miss:
'T was nectar both to taste and smell;
  I 'm love-drunk with that kiss.

Anonymous

13

Gurgling Jug, one-ear'd, long-throated,
                    buxom, neat, and high of chin,
Why be drunk when I am sober,
                    out of drink when I am in?
Bacchus' tapstress, Love's procuress,
                    maid-in-waiting to the Muse,
Smiling cateress of carousals,
                    why the toper's laws abuse?

Anonymous

14

There 's a hubbub at the cross,
   Mother Cypris, don't you see?
All who 've borne a lover's loss
   Have giv'n Love into custody.

Menecrates

Ere Age is ours we pray for it;
When 't is, we 've nought to say for it.

13 the toper's laws: *against being sober among the tipsy.*

[26]

Bion

The Muses fear not cruel Love, but aye
Their hearts befriend him and their feet waylay;
If one that hath not love within him sing,
They shrink from him and grudge their tutoring;
Should music come of one that 's love-possess'd,
Hotfoot they fly to aid him of their best.
I know that this is true; for I may praise
Other, or God or man, and my tongue stays,
Falt'ring; but if 't is Love and Lycidas,
My voice flows glad and glib as never 't was.

Meleâger

I

TO ZENOPHILA

Thou sleepest, pretty dear; and O
    Would I had come to-night,
Like the wing'd Sleep-God, wingless though,
    Upon thy lids to light!

The eyelids e'en of Zeus on high
    Give in to that sweet elf;
But thine he 'd leave alone, for I
    Should keep thee for myself.

1 wingless: *compare the Temple of the Wingless Victory, as of a victory that would abide.*

[27]   D 2

2

Sweet, ah, too sweet, Zenophilè,
The music of thy lute to me:
Where can I fly? Loves all around me
Pester, fluster, and confound me;
Here shoots thy beauty, here thy art,
Thy grace here, here—thy ev'ry part;
Each and all, they launch desire,
And where they hit they light a fire.

3

OF ZENOPHILA

The cup rejoiceth (well it may rejoice)
To 've touch'd the lips that blab my lov'd one's voice;
O that she put those lips to mine, and quaff'd,
Fond maid, the soul within me at a draught!

4

TO PHANION ('LITTLE BRAND')

Love 's pierced me with no shaft of his, nor lit
A torch, as erst, to fire my breast with it;
But brought the fellow-reveller of Desire,
Cypris' sweet brand, and touch'd my eyes with fire:
I 'm ashes now; that *little brand*, thy name,
Burnt in my breast; 't was spiritual flame.

2 & 4 *The arrows of the* Loves *or* Cupids *were fire-darts such as were used in war for firing an enemy's ships or stockades.*

[28]

Meleâger

5

Help, help! my maiden voyage o'er,
No sooner landed safe from sea and storm,
    Than Love must drag me from the shore
To light me hither to a lovely form.

I print its footmarks each with mine,
And seize and kiss the air 't yet seems to fill;
    Have I but 'scaped yon bitter brine
To cross another sea that 's bitterer still?

6

OF DÊMO

Break-of-day, the lover's foe,
Why round the world dost wheel so slow,
While in those slender arms doth lie
Another mate? yet when 'twas I
They clasp'd, thy light would haste the morrow
As 't were glad to see my sorrow.

7

OF HELIODÔRA

Like Gods that more than one God be,
My fair is writ in aspects three;
Persuasion 's first and Cypris second,
A sweet-tongued Grace for third is reckon'd:
For each of these one ladle pour;
I 'll drink it neat to Heliodore.

7 Persuasion (*Peitho*) *was the handmaid of* Cypris *or Aphrodite.*

8

Thou briny wave of Love, ye Jealousies
That blow for aye o'er Revel's stormy seas,
My rudder 's lost; O whither take ye me?
Shall I live yet my Scylla-love to see?

9

The die is cast. Boy, light the link.
Forward!
      —What would you, you in drink?
—I 'm after joy.
      —Joy? whither, pray?
—Argue with love? Light up, I say.
—Where 's all your lore of word and wit?
—'T was waste of time; away with it!
One thing I know, and that is, Love
Masters the might of Zeus above.

10

No wonder Love's are bolts that burn,
  His looks and laughter harsh: his mother
By Fire espous'd, by War belov'd,
  Owes just as much to one as t' other,
His grandam storms when winds blow high,
  His father 's nobody out of nought;
War's darts, Fire's flame, the Sea's quick ire—
  He hath them all, and so he ought.

10 Love *or Cupid was the child of Aphrodite, who was born of the sea and was the wife of the Fire-God and the mistress of the War-God.*

Meleáger

OF HELIODÔRA

Wine ho! and say 'to Heliodore',
  Say, and lift ladles one, two, three;
With that name mix'd and nothing more
  'T will make the sweet'st of drinks for me.

And bring that wreath to mind me of her,
  Wet with scents of yesterday;
Look! the rose that loves the lover
  Weeps to find my love away.

12

Now bloweth daffodil that loves the rain,
  Now bloweth lily, haunter of the hill,
Now bloweth violet so white again,
  And now blows one that loves her lover still.

Now blows a flow'r of all the flow'rs the best,
  Persuasion's own sweet rose, Zenophilè;
Why laugh ye, meads, in this your trimness dress'd?
  My darling 's more than all your sweets to me.

13

Cruel Love, beware, I pray,
  The soul that flutters round thee now:
If thou scorch her, she 'll away;
  She hath wings as well as thou.

13 *In the Greek the word for* soul *also means* butterfly.

Meleâger

14

Morning Star that bring'st the day,
Fare thee well, and quickly, pray,
Turn'd Ev'ning Star, when none may see,
Bring back the maid thou tak'st from me.

15

LOVE AT AUCTION

Still sleeping in his mother's lap, for sale!
    For sale! Why should I have this imp to keep?
Snub-nos'd and wing'd, and scratcheth with his nail,
    And then laughs most when most a' seems to weep;
And more, he 's malapert and rude, this child,
    Will have his way, talks without end or aim,
And sees when least ye think it; he 's so wild
    His very mother cannot make him tame,
A monster! So I 'll sell it. Is there not
    Some outbound merchant lacks a brat? Yet see
How 't weeps to stay! Thou shalt. Withdraw this lot.
    Take heart; I 'll rear thee with Zenophilè.

Zônas

Give me the earthen cup, 't is best of all:
Clay gave me birth, and will give burial.

15 lacks a brat: *to sell again to a slave-dealer.*

Philodêmus

I

Paphian Dêmo first I lov'd;
    That was just what would be:
Samian Dêmo was the next;
    That was as it should be:
But Naxian Dêmo, no joke that;
    And as for Argive Dêmo,—
If Philodêmus is my name,
    Fate call'd me what I seem-o.

2

OF CALLISTION

Friend of the joys of darkness, Queen of Night,
Shine through the lattice with your crescent light;
Illume my golden lass: what lovers do
Immortals may behold, and such are you.
I know you bless both her and me, good Moon;
Your heart was fired by young Endymion.

3

Seven and thirty years have gone,
    Torn from my life's book page by page;
My head, which grayer hairs hath grown,
    Warns me that wisdom comes with age.

Still burns this lover's longing heart,
    This serenader's string thrums on;
Muse, to the book's less serious part
    Write 'Catharine' for colophon.

3 *For* Catharine *the Greek has* Xanthippè, *and for* colophon corônis, *an elaborate flourish used by scribes to mark the end of a poem or* '*book*'.

4

O the foot of her! O the leg of her!
  O the thighs that have bid me die!
O her waist, and what 's below it!
  Her paps, throat, arms! her madding eye!
Those 'witching ways, that supreme kiss,
That prattle I 'd rather be hang'd than miss!—
She 's Roman—Flora is her name,
  She sings no song of Sappho's: granted;
Andromeda from India came,
  Yet Perseus found her what he wanted.

5

I 've lov'd: who hasn't? sung a serenade:
Well, who is not past master of that trade?
Run love-mad: ay, God-ridd'n. Away with it!
Gray hairs have read a lesson to my wit;
We play'd when it was playtime, I and you;
Now that it 's past, we 've better things to do.

⌘

4 prattle: *the Greek probably means 'baby-talk', or the love-talk of one
who speaks 'with an accent' and so suggests it.* Andromeda,
*generally described as a daughter of the king of Ethiopia, was rescued
from a sea-monster by Perseus son of Danaë, the great hero of Argos.*

Apollonidas

Old Euphron tills no many-furrow'd field,
No vineyard wide to me its fruit doth yield;
'T is but a shallow soil my ploughshare scrapes,
Nor is my wine the juice of myriad grapes:
Little of little comes; yet if so be
God give me more, He shall have more of me.

Anonymous

15

AN EPITAPH

As you pass by Anacreon's grave, good sir,
Pour a libation; he 's a wine-bibber.

Anonymous

16

CRABBED AGE

What 's left when wine runs low in jar
   Turns vinegar;
What 's left when life in man runs low
   Goes sour alsò.

[35]

Anonymous

17

PRAXITELES' STATUE OF APHRODITE AT CNIDUS

Paris, Adonis, and Anchîses,
    If I remember, only these
Have seen me naked: by what devices
    Has Praxiteles?

Evênus

THE TAUNT OF THE VINE

Though thou devour me to the root,
Yet will my stump bear so much fruit
As will make thy sacring, Goat,
When the knife is at thy throat.

Crinagoras

TO HIMSELF

Turn as you will, to right or left,
Crinagoras, on your bed bereft,
With no Gemella to you press'd
You 've gone to bed but not to rest.

EVÊNUS: *Found not only in the* Palatine Anthology *but as the caption of a wall-painting at Pompeii.*

[36]

Marcus Argentarius

I

THE POET'S DEDICATION TO APHRODITE

Tipsy, daft, and babbling Bottle,
     fellow-guest where cronies sup,
Slim-neck'd daughter of the club-feast,
     sister of the ambrosial cup,
Self-taught serving-maid of mortals,
     willing tool of mirth and wine,
Sweetest mystagogue of lovers,
     rest for ever in Love's shrine;
Here to Love's great God devoted,
     with this paean in thy praise,
Rest, sweet sot, where grateful Marcus
     leaves the old comrade of his ways.

2

Sing no more, Blackbird, perch'd atop yon tree;
The oak is no fit singing-place for thee:
Go where the vine doth sprout her gray-green shade;
Hers is the branch should stay thy tiny feet,
From her should come thy call so shrill and sweet:
The oak 's thy foe; birdlime, the fowler's aid,
Comes of the oak; 't is grapes come of the vine:
Singers are friends with the great God of Wine.

---

2 gray-green *is the colour of the half-unfolded vine leaf.*   *They made* birdlime *of mistletoe.*

Marcus Argentarius

3

Lend me a hand, some kind friend, do;
    I 'm reeling drunk; the wine was neat:
Bacchus, play fair; I carry you,
    You carry me—but off my feet.

4

Six feet of earth will soon be thine,
    And then good-bye to light and life;
Be merry, Cincius; quaff sheer wine,
    Thy arms around thy pretty wife:
Think'st thou wisdom will abide?
Zêno and Cleanthes died.

Antiphilus

1

Of Cynthia's baby charms I said
'When she 's grown up she 'll kill us dead':
They laugh'd; the time is come, and lo!
I was wounded long ago.

What can I do? when I come nigh her,
To avoid is pain, to view is fire;
Yet if I sue, 't is 'Maid am I':
True to my prophecy I die.

---

4 Zêno and Cleanthes: *the great Stoics.*   1 Cynthia *in the Greek*
is Tereina.

Antiphilus or Philodêmus

2

Wait, my dainty one, wait, and say
  What your pretty name may be;
Where can we meet? Of course, I 'll pay
  Whatever you like. Not speak to me?

Where do you live, then, tell me, do;
  I 'll send to fetch you. You 've to meet
Somebody else? it can't be true:
  Well, here 's Good-night to you, Miss Conceit.

No Good-night for *me*? I 'll try
  Again and again, then; why, I 've often
  Had harder hearts than yours to soften:
Just for the present, though, Good-bye.

Maecius

OF HEDYLION; TO APHRODITE

I swore by Thee, Great Queen above,
Two nights I would not meet my love;
Methinks Thou smiledst then, as who
Well my poor heart's ailment knew:
One night I 've borne; the winds may take
My oath for t' other; for her sake
I 'd liefer far break pledge with Thee
Than keep 't and die of piety.

Nicarchus

If I must die, what though with gouty toe
Or foot as fleet as hares' I pass below?
Many 's the hand will lift; lame me or not,
'T is all one to the sexton; fill the pot!

✦

Strato

TO DAMOCRATES

Now 's the time to drink, lad,
   And now 's the time to woo;
Neither time 's for ever
   For either me or you.

Our brows be sweet with roses,
   Our bosoms with perfumes,
Before the mourners bring them
   For off'rings at our tombs.

Better my bones should get their wine
   While flesh is on them still;
When I am dead, the Deluge
   Can take them if it will.

✦

STRATO: *After cremation wine was poured over the unburnt bones.*

Rufīnus

1

I 'm arm'd with Reason 'gainst Sir Love,
    And God 'gainst man he shall not win;
But if Squire Wine take up the glove,
    'T is two to one, and I give in.

2

TO PRODICÈ

Come let us bathe, and flow'rs for chaplets twine,
Then fill great cups and quaff unwater'd wine:
Brief is our life of joyance; soon, sweet friend,
Old Age will come to thwart and Death to end.

❧

Anonymous or Rufīnus

18

Ten Muses are there, Aphroditès two,
And Graces four, dear Dercylis, with you;
In each sweet sort of godhead you 've a place,
As Muse, as Aphroditè, and as Grace.

❧

Anonymous

19

Drink and be merry; what the morn will bring
No man can tell. Sweat not, but have your fling;
Be human; give, share, eat, whate'er you can:
'Twixt live and live-not there 's but little span;
All life 's the turn of a scale which hairs incline;
If you 're in time, all 's yours, if late, 't is mine.

Lucian

1

A bad man 's like a leaky cask to fill;
Keep pouring kindness in, he 's empty still.

2

TO CAUTIOUS

Sober for choice amidst a drunken crew,
You look'd as if no one were drunk but you.

Palladas

1

I 'm the laugh of every lass
Who points me to the looking-glass
And says 'See what you 've come to'; yet,
Be my locks of snow or jet,
I take the graybeard's anodyne
Of roses, ambergris, and wine.

[42]

Palladas

2

All human kind the debt of death must pay;
None knows at night whether he 'll live till day:
Learn this, and make thee merry, fellow-man;
Drown thoughts of death in many a cup and can,
Take toll of Love while life is still on tap,
And leave all else to rest in Fortune's lap.

3

Life 's but life, and that 's good living;
Cares, avaunt! we 're busy men:
Come, let 's take when Fate 's a-giving,
      Dancing, drinking,
      Loving, linking;
Now we know, there 's doubt of *Then*.

4

When in the daybook of my memory
I reckon up my losses on life's 'change
And note the random width of Fortune's range
And how she giveth ease to Poverty
And dispossesseth Wealth of his estate,
Then, dazed for my lone wand'ring o'er the sheets,
I curse my ciph'rings, they 're so hard to rate;
For how shall I get even with this dame,
Who springs out God knows whence in life's dark streets,
Strumpet by nature if she 's wife in name?

Anonymous

20

In the green grape you said no;
In the black you bade me go:
In the dry, be kinder, do,
And give me just a taste of you.

❧

Leontius

FOR A GIFT TO HIS LADY

To the lip with you, good cup;
You 've found honey; lap it up:
I don't grudge what you 'll enjoy;
Yet O to have your luck, my boy!

❧

Eratosthenes

A DEDICATION

This wine-cask void of wine
   Gave Xenophon, the sot:
Be kind, Lord of the Vine;
   He gave Thee all he 'd got.

[44]

Macedonius the Consul

FOR AN INN

Native or not you 're a friend to me;
'T is not true hospitality
To ask who, whose, or whence you be.

2

Give me not gold nor earth's ten thousand cities,
The wealth of Homer's Thebes to me is nought;
Put me where company of worth and wit is,
Where wine that other men may sweat to win
Brims the fat bowl, and streams that know no drought
Flow for the lip to bathe and linger in:
That 's wealth for me; when I the wine-cup hold,
A fig for your great consuls and their gold!

3

TO EVIPPÈ

A neatherd who saw Niobè
   Wonder'd that living rock should weep;
A living rock you are to me,
   While sad this long dark watch I keep:
Love is to blame for my grief too;
She lov'd her children, I love you.

3 Niobè *was changed to a dripping rock for boasting of the number of her children.*

[45]

4

I dreamt I clasp'd her in my arms,
    My laughter-loving Mary;
She offer'd freely of her charms—
    Nor coy was she nor chary.

But a jealous Love laid wait, it seems,
    Who upset all my blisses,
And woke me: Love e'en in my dreams
    Grudges me more than kisses.

5

I pray thee respite, Love, for my poor heart;
If shoot thou wilt, shoot at some other part.

6

Ye who to Bacchus' joyful rites give heed,
Take heart of grace from wine, and cast out Need;
A mixing-bowl for cup, Heav'n give me that,
And for a cask a mirth-enshrining vat!
Then, when of my dear drink I've had my fill,
I'll fight the very Giants if you will:
I dread nor thunderbolts nor ruthless sea;
Bacchus is courage, and he'll be in me.

4 *The Greek gives no name.*

Macedonius the Consul

7

Do Love no despite, Star that bring'st the Morn,
Nor of thy warlike neighbour learn to scorn
What calls for pity; but as years agone,
When thou saw'st Clymenè with Phaëthon,
Thou stay'dst thy course as soon as thou wast bright,
So after this dear hardly-hoped-for night
With lagging lustre let thy race be run,
As in the land where Winter sees no sun.

❦

Paul the Silentiary

I

Think, Cleophantis, how that bliss you 'd name,
When the great wind of love doth equal blow
On two fond hearts; no war, no dread, no shame,
Can loose their dear entwinement: I would bear
The Lemnos-forgèd nets of long ago
And all the Fire-God's devilish craft could do,
So I might knit my two arms round my dear,
And have my heart's content of all that 's you.
Came such luck my way, then upon my life,
Let see who would, friend, stranger, priest, or wife.

7 *The reference is to the planets Venus and Mars.*   1 *The reference is to the netting of Ares and Aphrodite by her outraged husband, the Blacksmith-God Hephaestus, and the way the other Gods stood round the bed and laughed, as Homer tells.*

Paul the Silentiary

2

Cleophantis cometh not;
   The lamp (it is the third I 've lit)
Flickers; I would the flame that 's hot
   Within my heart might die with it
And let me sleep! How often, though,
   She swore by Love whate'er the odds
To come at nightfall! Now I know
   She recketh nought of men nor Gods.

3

Nancy's kiss is loud and long,
   Jenny's soft and tender,
Marian's hurts, it is so strong;
   Which loan best pays the lender?

Ears can't decide such suits as this;
   Taste 's the judge to do it.—
Well, heart, you 're wrong; Jane's dewy kiss
   Is honey-sweet, you knew it.

Keep to your choice; she 's won the day,
   And bribed me ne'er a penny;
No lad who 'd look another way
   Shall draw me from my Jenny.

3 *In the Greek the names are* Galatea, Dêmo, *and* Doris.

[48]

Paul the Silentiary

4

Here 's from us topers to the Mirthmaker,
A bumper that shall outlaw murderous Care:
The sweating delver his bread-battening maw
May cram with Pluto's dismal Mother-in-law;
Beef's oxen-butchering blood-begotten feasts
We 'll leave to carrion birds and ravening beasts;
And fishbones that can cut them like a knife
Be theirs who think that death 's as good as life:
Us bounteous wine in meat and drink shall keep;
So nectar 's ours, ambrosia may go cheap.

5

With one hair from her golden head
    Doll bound my wrists and took me;
'Easy lost if easy led'
    Methought, and laughter shook me.

But tugging only made me cry;
    'T was like an iron fetter:
Now, hair-hung, whitherso'er she try
    To draw me, I must let her.

4 *For* Pluto's Mother-in-law *the Greek has* Persephone's Mother
(*Dêmêter, Goddess of Corn*).   5 *For* Doll *the Greek has* Doris.

E   [49]   G

Paul the Silentiary

6

OF A GAY LADY

Coaxing Kit, my thought 's with Jack,
  Kissing Jack, with John,
Hugging John, to Kit flies back;
  Him I have gets none.

Thus to love's wealth I steal my way,
  And make a pretty picking;
Love-poor let all who blame me stay,
  To one mate ever sticking.

Agathias

I love not wine; yet if thou 'dst make
  A sad man merry, sip first sup,
  And when thou giv'st I 'll take the cup:
If thy lip touch it, for thy sake
  No more may I be stiff and staid
  And the luscious jug evade:
The cup convoys thy kiss to me,
And tells the joy it had of thee.

6 *In the Greek the names are* Hippomenes, Leander, *and* Xanthus.

[50]

Irenaeus the Referendary

You 've given in, proud Margery,
　You 've ceas'd to flaunt and flout me;
A willing prisoner I lie
　With your sweet arms about me:
Thus souls, thus bodies, join their flow,
And in Love's river onward go.

Anonymous or Rufinus

21

Sweet to the sweet I send you, lady mine,
Perfume, as wine pour'd to the God of Wine.

The Sources of the Poems

A.P. = *Anthologia Palatina*, *Plan.* its Planudean Appendix, *L.G.* = *Lyra Graeca* in the Loeb Classical Library, *E.I.* = *Elegy and Iambus* in the same, Dl. = Diehl *Anthologia Lyrica* in the Teubner series; for the Palatine Anthology and Appendix see Paton *Greek Anthology* in the Loeb Classical Library, and, for Books i–ix of the same, Stadtmüller *Anthologia Graeca Epigrammatum* in the Teubner series (subtracting one from all references to Book v); for the later Books, and Epigrams preserved elsewhere, see also Dübner *Anthologia Palatina etc.* in the Didot series.

Notes on the Text

Emendations marked *E* the translator believes to be his own.

Sappho 1: Reading ἄβραις for ἁβροῖς with Blomfield, and τοῖς
ἐταίροις τοίσδεσ' ἔμοις (*E*) for τούτοισι τοῖς ἐταίροις
ἐμοῖς; an alternative is to read the feminine and suppose the
gender to have been changed to suit the quoter's company in
Athenaeus.

    2: Reading πέρθεσσ(ο) for πάρθεσθ' (mss) or]ερθεσ[(pap.)
and γὰρ παρπέλεται καὶ Χάριτας μάκαιρας for γὰρ πέλεται
καὶ Χάριτες μάκαιρα (*E*); προτέρην = προσορᾶν (Seidler).

Solon: After line 4 an early addition *in mal. part.* is found in
the mss: 'of lad or lass; and when the time for these things is
come and youth is accordant (*or* of lad and lass, and when
youth is come thus far, and with the right age they are fitting
pleasures).'

Alcaeus 1: Reading ἄϊτ', ἀπ' οἴκιδος for αἱ τὰ ποικίλα or ποι-
κίλλις (*E*); others read ἄϊτα, ποικίλαις.

    2: Supplying ἐπιδενδρίων after τέττιξ from Jul. *Ep.* 24 (*E*).

Cleobûlus: If this is as early as Cleobûlus the alternatives are δὶς
τριάκοντα and ἑξήκοντα; the former *may* be an emendation
made after *a* had become short, but the variation between
παῖδες and κοῦραι is in favour of its being original (cf.
Δαμαρετίου Simon. 170, *L.G.* ii, Dl. 106b), and it makes a
better point.

Ibycus: Reading βαλεῖ or βαλέϊ for βάλλει (*E*).

Demodocus: Imitated by Porson: 'The Germans at Greek are
sadly to seek, | ... All except Hermann, | And Hermann's a
German.'

Theognis 8: Reading with Bergk ἥβᾳ for ἥβης, and in line 5 καλόν
for κακόν.

    10: Reading ὅτε πρῶτ' (*E*) for ὃν πρῶτ', and ἔτ' ἀειρόμενος
with Herwerden for ἐσαειράμενος.

    11: Reading ὥστε κάμ' ὑδρείῳ (*E*) for ὥσθ' ἅμα ὑδρεύει, which
makes the word-order impossible, and Hermann's βαλὼν
for λαβών.

NOTES ON THE TEXT

Anacreon 2: Reading Μούσας for Μουσέων (*E*); otherwise the word-order is impossible.

    4: Reading δεξιὸς γὰρ ἱπποπείρης ὣν ἔχω σ' ἀνεμβάτην (*E*) for δεξιὸν γὰρ ἱπποπείρην οὐχ ἕξεις ἐπεμβάτην, which requires ἐγώ in line 3.

Athenian Drinking-Song 4: Perhaps πίνειν δ' ἀμυστί (*E*) was the original of Ameipsias' σὺ δὲ κάρτ' ἀφειδής, 'but you're too greedy'.

Simonides 2: From Ammianus Marcellinus 14. 6. 7: 'ut enim Simonides lyricus docet, beate perfecta ratione victuro ante alia patriam esse convenit gloriosam.'

    3: Reading σύν (adverb, *E*) for νῦν, θεᾶν (*E*) for θυάν, χορόν with Wilamowitz for χῶρον, and πάντως (*E*) for πάντων.

    4: French could do it better.

    5: Reading τῇ with Casaubon for τήν, ὀξύς with Valckenaer for ὠκύς, and ἐθάφθη with Porson for ἐκάμφθη.

Timocreon: Reading σὲ γὰρ δή.

Anonymous 3: Reading with Jacobs εἰ καὶ ἔφυσαν for οὐκ ἐνέφυσαν.

Callistratus: Reading ποδώκη τ' Ἀχιλέα Τυδείδην τ' ἔτ' ἐσθλὸν Διομήδεα (*E*) for ποδώκης Ἀχιλλεὺς Τυδείδην τέ φασι τὸν ἐσθλὸν Διομήδεα.

Thales (?): Reading ἔν τέ τι (*E*) for ἔν τι.

Solon (?): Reading φαιδρῷ σε with Bergk for φαιδρῶ.

Cheilon (?): Reading ἐν δὲ χρόνῳ with Headlam for ἐν δὲ χρυσῷ.

Pittacus (?): Reading ἐπὶ φῶτα for ποτὶ φῶτα with the edition of Froben, and ἔχουσι for ἔχουσα with Bergk.

Bias (?): Reading πολλάκι δή for πολλάκι with C. F. Hermann.

Asclepiades 1: This makes a single poem with 4 in the mss; I follow Mackail in separating them.

    2: ὑψοῦ seems corrupt, and I read συμφέρεται (subject εἶς) for συμφέρομαι, and, with Jacobs, δ' εἰς ἑνί for δίσσενί. Damis is a masculine name, but the use of two masculines in the last line does not preclude my interpretation.

    4: Reading in line 3 δύσερως with Kaibel for οὐ γὰρ ἔρως.

    5: Supplying ἔπειγε after πρόσλαβε with Stadtmüller.

    6: For ὡς ἂν ἄμεινον I suggest ὡς ἀμερίμνου; a name, with αὐτόν preceding, is impossible.

Anonymous 10: Reading with Hecker φιλοκώμοις παννυχίσιν for φιλόκωμος παννύχιος.

Meleâger 2: Reading with Reiske πάντα· πυρὶ φλέγομαι.

    5: Reading ἀπέστρεψεν (*E*) for ἀπεστρέπτει in line 4.

13: Reading with Hecker περινηχομένην for πυρὶ νηχομένην.

15: Reading with Lobeck λιρόν for λοιπόν in line 5.

Philodêmus 1: Reading Ναξιακῆς with Kaibel in line 3 where the mss are corrupt.

4: Reading in line 6 (with Ellis) θῦ' ἐμέ (mss. θύεμε or κλῶμαι) as an adjective of high praise; it must have been a colloquial phrase, 'sacrifice me!', implying willingness to do anything in order to get; compare μηρῶν τῶν ἀπόλωλα δικαίως above, where τῶν is the article and ἀπόλωλα δικαίως is used as an adjective, as it were 'fitly-died-for thighs' or 'life-well-lost-for thighs', both alternative translations which the translator shrank from printing in his text; compare Shakespeare's 'the world-without-end hour', *Sonnet* 57, πῶς δοκεῖς as an adverb, and, an extreme instance, ὀρχηστρίδες τὰ φίλταθ' Ἁρμοδίου καλαί, Ar. *Ach.* 1093, where the words of the song, φίλταθ' Ἁρμόδι' οὔ (τί που τέθνηκας) do duty as 'very'.

Apollonidas: Reading εἶσιν for εἰ μὴ δ' with Stadtmüller.

Anonymous 16: Reading εἰς ὄξος with Hermann for εἰς ὀξύ.

Nîcarchus: Reading with Meineke ἀροῦσιν in line 3 and γὰρ ἴδ' ὡς in line 4.

Palladas 4: Taking ἄκαιροι μεταβολαί as 'bad bargains' at business, see the new Liddell and Scott *s.* μεταβολή.

Paul the Silentiary 1: Reading with Jacobs βοσκόμενος for βουλόμενος in line 9.

Irenaeus the Referendary: Reading ψυχαί (*E*) for ψυχή, and no comma after συμφέρεται. (For 'Margery' the Greek has 'Rhodopè.')

✠

[59]

Index of the Poets

WITH DATES AND SOURCES

The date is the *floruit*, about the 40th year. References are given
on pp. 53 ff.

[61]

English Index of First Words

with references to the second edition of Mackail's *Select Epigrams from the Greek Anthology* and the *Oxford Book of Greek Verse*.

[63]

E [65]

Greek Index of First Words

[68]

GREEK INDEX OF FIRST WORDS